FUN READING ABOUT 【悦读中国】
CHINA
Chinese Folk Arts and Crafts

Su Gang

740-GAN

Huang Shan Publishing House

图书在版编目(CIP)数据

民间工艺美术：英文 /苏刚编著; 庞咪咪译. -- 合肥：黄
山书社, 2014.1
（悦读中国）
ISBN 978-7-5461-2051-5

Ⅰ. ①民… Ⅱ. ①苏… ②庞… Ⅲ. ①民间工艺—中国—
通俗读物—英文 Ⅳ. ①J528-49

中国版本图书馆CIP数据核字(2013)第319402号

悦读中国：民间工艺美术
YUE DU ZHONG GUO :MIN JIAN GONG YI MEI SHU   苏　刚 编著

出 版 人：任耕耘
策　 划：任耕耘　蒋一谈
责任编辑：司　雯
责任印制：戚　帅　李　磊   装帧设计：商子庄

出版发行：时代出版传媒股份有限公司（http://www.press-mart.com）
　　　　　黄山书社（http://www.hsbook.cn）
　　　　　官方直营书店网址（http://hsssbook.taobao.com）
　　　　　营销部电话：0551—63533762　63533768
　　　　　（合肥市政务文化新区翡翠路1118号出版传媒广场7层　邮编：230071）
经　　销：新华书店
印　　刷：安徽联众印刷有限公司

开本：710×875　1/16　　　　　印张：7　　　　　　　字数：90千字
版次：2014年4月第1版　　　　印次：2014年4月第1次印刷
书号：ISBN　978-7-5461-2051-5　　　　　　　　　　定价：58.00元

Foreword

What kind of Chinese arts and crafts attracts you the most? Is it the exquisite embroidery, the colorful woodblock Chinese New Year paintings, the red Chinese paper cuts or decorative knots, the elegant blue-and-white Chinese porcelain, the Chinese kites of different shapes or the artistic Yixing purple clay teapots?

For thousands of years, the Chinese people created numerous world renowned artworks demonstrating the unique Chinese cultural characteristics and charm. Let us guide you into the colorful world of Chinese folk arts and crafts nurtured in the Chinese civilization.

Contents

Folk Arts 1

2 Folk Crafts

Folk Arts

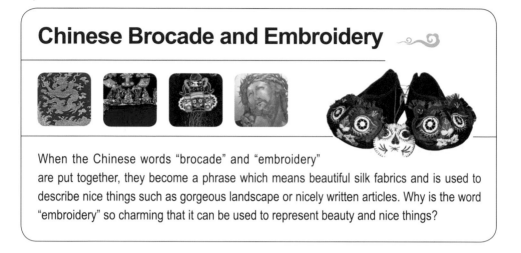

Chinese Brocade and Embroidery

When the Chinese words "brocade" and "embroidery"
are put together, they become a phrase which means beautiful silk fabrics and is used to
describe nice things such as gorgeous landscape or nicely written articles. Why is the word
"embroidery" so charming that it can be used to represent beauty and nice things?

A Popular Folk Art from the Imperial Family

Embroidery is a handicraft of
creating ornamental designs
on fabrics with needles and
threads. Chinese embroidery has a history
of several thousand years. Originated as a special
handicraft of the imperial families, embroidered
silk garments, out of reach for ordinary people,
were only enjoyed by emperors and dignitaries.
The emperor as the highest ruler of the country

◆ Qing Dynasty Emperor Qianlong's Dragon
Robe of Yellow Silk Satin Embroidered with
Patterns of Mythical Bats

usually chose the dragon image as the central emblem for his robe. All emperors in the Zhou Dynasty wore embroidered dragon robes with patterns of the sun, the moon, stars, dragon and fire. In the Ming and Qing Dynasties, embroidery designs in the imperial court dressing became an important representation of rankings for officials, with birds for civil officials and animals for military officers.

Embroidery gradually flourished as a folk handcraft for ordinary people to use as decorations on their clothes and other daily necessities such as sachets, tobacco pouches, pillowcases, tablecloths, and chair cushions. The embroidery technique reached its height in the Qing Dynasty with highly sophisticated stitches and rich patterns.

◆ **Shoes Embroidered with A Tiger Head**
Shoes embroidered with a tiger head are hand made Chinese traditional children's shoes. In the Chinese folk culture, tigers are perceived as the king of all beasts. The embroidery of a tiger head on the shoes is considered as a blessing for the child.

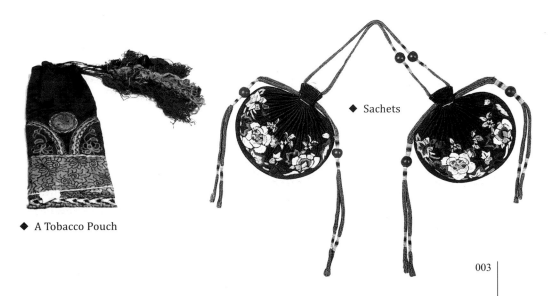

◆ Sachets

◆ A Tobacco Pouch

Women's Specialized Needlework

Chinese women's needlework generally refers to weaving, sewing and embroidery. In ancient China men must be good at farming and women must learn needlework from childhood. The quality of a woman's needlework became an important criterion to determine if she was virtuous.

Under the influence of the traditional culture many Chinese women developed superb needlework techniques in using tiny needles to create very complicated and elegant patterns, images and calligraphy. During the Three Kingdoms Period, the legendary Madame Zhao of King Wu was said to be able to embroider a silk topography of various kingdoms in the most famous five mountainous regions of China. Lu Mei, a fourteen-year-old Tang Dynasty girl, embroidered seven volumes of the "Lotus

◆ Shen Shou's Embroidery "The Portrait of Jesus"

◆ Shen Shou's Embroidery "The Portrait of Italian Queen"

Sutra" on one-foot long silk scroll with very fine miliary-size words. Shen Shou, a Qing Dynasty woman, developed a world-renown style of her own known as simulated embroidery based on real-life objects or people.

Four Famous Embroidery Styles

Over many centuries, various regional areas became known for their distinctive styles of embroidery including the most famous four of Suzhou, Hunan, Guangdong and Sichuan embroidery in addition to other unique styles from Miao, Yi and Dong ethnic minorities.

◆ Beijing Embroidery of a Silk Curtain with Images of Children Playing, Qing Dynasty

Su embroidery from Suzhou, Jiangsu Province is mainly used for interior decorations with its elegant colors, intricate designs and a variety of stitches all executed in the most meticulous manner and craftsmanship. The double-sided embroidery produced by the most skillful masters is considered one of the best artworks. Hunan embroidery from areas around Changsha, Hunan

◆ Hunan Embroidery of Flowers and Birds

◆ Su Embroidery of a Cat

Province uses silk velvet threads to create a distinctive style of color and shadow contrast using Chinese traditional ink paintings as blueprints. The velvet surface of this kind of embroidery work produces a bold realistic effect. Guangdong embroidery from Guangzhou, Guangdong Province is famous for its vibrant colors and sophisticated stitches. Sichuan embroidery from Chengdu,

◆ Sichuan Embroidery of Paradise Flycatchers

◆ Guangdong Embroidery of Phoenixes

Sichuan Province has an emphasis on delicate stitching and natural appearances.

The embroidery work from the Miao ethnic group shows a visual effect that brings together different dimensions in a harmonious way with matching colors and irregular geometric patterns. The very unique

◆ Miao Embroidery of an Ornamental Shoulder Piece

cross-stitch embroidery from the Yi ethnic minority is mainly used as handmade accessories for women's clothing. One such dress can take one or two years to complete. The embroidered trims from the Dong ethnic group have exquisite patterns resembling motifs and its repeated stitches increase the durability of clothing.

◆ Miao Embroidery

Woodblock Chinese New Year Pictures

Chinese New Year pictures are an auspicious symbol, very popular decorations for the Chinese New Year celebrations.
During the Chinese New Year holidays, people post them on doors and hang them on walls to promote festivities and express good wishes for the coming year.

New Year Door Guardian Pictures

What is the story behind the Chinese tradition of hanging Door Guardian pictures for the Chinese New Year holidays?

The legend says Emperor Li Shiming of Tang Dynasty often felt sick as a result of ghost intrusions in his dreams. Two of his generals Qin Qiong and Yuchi Gong decided to stand outside of his palace to guard against evil spirits to enter his dreams. Later the emperor posted pictures of the two generals on the doors, which unexpectedly achieved the same effect. When the story became widespread among the people, the images of these two

◆ Chinese New Year Pictures
   on the Front Gate

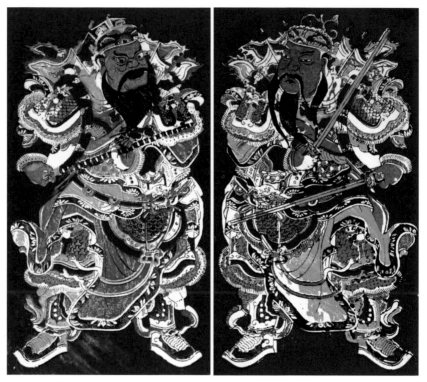

◆ New Year Door Guardian Pictures of Zhangzhou, Ming Dynasty

generals gradually became door guardians in pictures. During the Chinese New Year holidays, people like to hang their pictures on gates and doors in the hope of warding off evils and disasters.

Making a Chinese New Year Picture

Is a Chinese New Year picture painted individually? Certainly not. In ancient times Chinese New Year pictures were in high demand on New Year's Eve as many families wanted to buy them for the celebrations. Individual painters couldn't possibly meet such demand. Therefore people created a woodblock mold, brushed on it ink and pigments, and slightly pressed the paper onto the mold to make a print. The result was similar to the print made from the Chinese seal. The difference is that a Chinese New Year picture required various colors. One picture needed to go through multiple overlay printing processes on several molds.

Chinese New Year pictures printed with this technique are referred to as woodblock New Year pictures. The Japanese Ukiyo-e was deeply influenced by the Chinese woodblock printing.

◆ Qing Dynasty New Year Picture "A Birthday Celebration for Eight Immortals"

Good Wishes from New Year Pictures

While promoting festivities for New Year holidays, the Chinese New Year pictures also convey people's good wishes and aspirations for a better life in the coming year. The most popular themes include New Year blessings, year-after-year abundance and wealth, forever peace, promotions and salary increases. Pictures showing daily activities, traditional festivals, folk customs and interesting anecdotes are also very common. Well-known stories from local operas are clearly evident in regional New Year pictures of strong local flavors. The artistic connotations embedded in such New Year pictures help to promote folk literature heritage and dissemination.

◆ New Year Picture "Year-after-year Abundance"
This New Year picture "Year-after-year Abundance" shows a child, a fish and some lotus flowers. The Chinese words for fish and lotus flowers are homonymic to words for "Year-after-year" and "Abundance." This picture metaphorically depicts a prosperous life year after year.

◆ "Yanmen Town of Suzhou", a Qing Dynasty New Year Picture of Taohuawu, Suzhou

One New Year Picture, One Story

◆ "General Zhao Yun Saved the Prince"
Zhao Yun was a famous general in the Three Kingdoms Period. Once in a battle he was responsible for protecting the King of Shu in a retreat and discovered that the prince was missing in the chaos. He risked his own life and returned to the battlefield with some of his soldiers. By the time the prince was found, all but the general himself were dead. The general fought his way out of the siege carrying the prince on his back and returned him safely to the king.

◆ "Mother Educates the Son"
It is said that in the Ming Dynasty a woman raised her son alone after the death of her husband. One day the son was ridiculed in the school and refused to go back to school. The woman was so angry that she broke the loom to show her determination not to let him give up his study. The son understood his mother's painstaking efforts to raise him and started to work very hard at school. He eventually became a talented scholar-official and returned to his hometown with fame and wealth.

◆ **"The Ruse of Empty City"**

In the Three Kingdoms Period, when a city of Kingdom Shu was in peril of being attacked by the greatly outnumbered Wei army, Shu's Chancellor Zhuge Liang calmly ordered to open the city gate and played music on the gate tower. The Wei army general was surprised by what he saw and suspected that there was an ambush inside the city. The Wei army didn't launch the attack and retreated immediately.

◆ **"The Weaving Fairy and the Cowherd"**

The weaving fairy and the cowherd are two characters in a Chinese ancient legend. The hardworking weaving fairy is said to be the granddaughter of the God of Heaven living in the east side of the Milky Way. Later she fell in love with the cowherd living on the west side of the Milky Way. The God of Heaven approved their marriage. But after they got married, the weaving fairy neglected her weaving work. The God of Heaven became so furious that he ordered her to return to the east side and only allowed her to see the cowherd once a year at the magpie bridge over the Milky Way on July the 7th of the Chinese lunar calendar.

◆ "Butterfly Lovers"

It is said the in the Western Jin Dynasty, a young scholar from a poor family fell in love with a girl from a rich family. The girl's family rejected the proposed marriage from the scholar and arranged her marriage with another rich and powerful family. As a result the young scholar became very sick and died in despair. On the day of the wedding, the girl insisted on getting down to pay her respect at the young scholar's grave. Suddenly, the grave cracked open and she threw herself into the grave to join the scholar. They turned into a pair of beautiful butterflies and flew away. Their story became a legend of faithful love in China.

Red Paper Cuts

Chinese paper cuts are a very popular folk art in the countryside. With a regular pair of scissors or a knife, rich patterns and unique images can magically emerge from an ordinary piece of color paper.

Joyful Paper Cuts

Chinese paper cuts have a variety of styles and can be made for windows, doors, lanterns and special occasions such as holidays, celebrations and weddings.

Paper cuts on windows are called "window flowers" in Chinese and used mainly for holidays and celebrations to express longings and pursuit for a good life. A rich variety of themes depicts a peasant's life in farming, sericulture, weaving, fishing and

◆ Window Paper Cuts

hunting, and animal husbandry. Others include images of auspicious flowers, plants and beasts. Window paper cuts can be posted individually, in pairs or in sets.

Paper cuts used in celebrations such as weddings, birthday or housewarming parties are known as "joyful flowers", with designs emphasizing cheerfulness and good luck. Common patterns are mostly auspicious Chinese characters such as longevity, blessing or double happiness.

Paper-cut streamers are hung over doors or on Buddhist shrines during the Chinese New Year holidays to promote joyfulness. They usually have a rectangular shape

◆ Different Wedding Paper Cuts

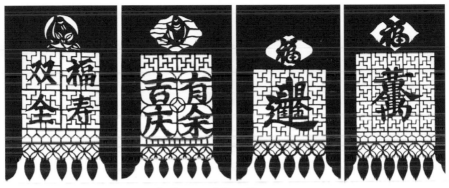

◆ Paper-cut Door Streamers

consisting of a center design, a frame and bottom tassels. The design in the center falls into two categories: flower patterns or auspicious characters.

"Lantern flowers" are paper cuts posted on lanterns, usually with pictures of folk stories, figures in local operas or Chinese characters implying wealth, longevity, bumper harvests or good weather, etc. When the candle inside the lantern is lit, the paper cut looks more vivid in the moving light.

Red color is used in most of the Chinese paper cuts for the color red symbolizes good luck and joyfulness in China. People like to use red paper cuts as decorations for holidays, weddings, childbirth celebrations, birthday parties, housewarming parties and openings of new businesses.

◆ Paper-cut Lantern

Chinese Zodiac Paper Cuts

Chinese zodiac represents the year of the birth, similar to the concept of Western astrology for the birth of the month.

It has a time circle of 12 years, each year labeled with an animal name. The twelve Chinese zodiac animal signs consist of rat, ox, tiger, rabbit, dragon, snake, horse, goat, monkey, rooster, dog and pig. For example, 2014 is the year of horse in the Chinese lunar calendar. Therefore all people who are born in this year belong to the zodiac sign of the horse. The Chinese believe that the zodiac sign stays with the person throughout his life and brings him lucky dates and opportunities.

The ancient Chinese selected these twelve animals based on their farming and life experience as well as their worship of animal totems. The twelve animals are divided into three categories. Ox, goat, horse, pig, dog and rooster are livestock symbolizing prosperity and good fortune of the family. Tiger, rabbit, monkey, rat and snake are wild animals that people know best and frequently have contact with. Dragon is the symbol of the Chinese culture and regarded as an auspicious beast representing power and good luck.

◆ Rat

◆ Ox

◆ Tiger

◆ Rabbit

◆ Dragon

◆ Snake

◆ Horse

◆ Goat

◆ Monkey

◆ Rooster

◆ Dog

◆ Pig

Paper Cuts Applications in Modern Life

Paper cuts are commonly found in the daily life of the Chinese people. During the Chinese New Year holidays, they are posted on the windows and hung over the doors in almost every home in the countryside for prosperity and good luck in the coming year. Homes of the newlyweds are also decorated everywhere with red paper cuts, which are usually made by women from the groom's family. In some places when she arrives at the groom's house, the bride is expected to bring her own paper-cut work as part of the dowry.

Today the paper-cut art has been applied to other fields. For example, fashion designers have integrated the techniques and patterns of the paper-cut art into their costume design to produce a hollow effect. Architects have also adopted some paper-cut design concepts into modern building structures.

Paper cuts have also been made into animated films. In 1985 the first paper-cut cartoon "Pig Bajie Eat Watermelons" was made in China. Since then several other paper-cut animated films came out in succession including "The Fox Hunts the Hunter", "The Monkey Fishes the Moon", "The Mouse Gets Daughter Married", "Gourd Brothers", "Fox Tricks the Crow" and "The Twelve Zodiac Signs", all of which were well-received by Chinese children.

◆ Chinese Cheongsam Dress with Paper-cut Design Patterns

How to Cut Chinese Word "Double Happiness"

The "double happiness" word is a traditional Chinese decorative pattern consisting of two characters of happiness connected together. Representing good luck and jubilation, this word pattern is widely used on bronze, porcelain, fabric, furniture, wood carvings, clothing, calligraphy, and particularly in paper cuts and Chinese New Year pictures to imply celebrations of double happiness.

The following are steps to cut a simple "double happiness" word pattern.

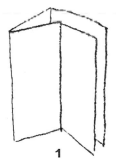

1. First prepare a piece of rectangular or square paper. Fold the paper in half horizontally and then fold it again in half so that it has four equal parts.

2. Trace the "double happiness" word pattern on the folded paper as shown in the illustration.

3. Cut out the dark shaded areas. Open it up and you have a "double happiness" paper cut.

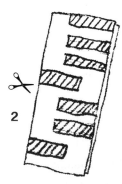

Carvings of Huizhou

Huizhou is a historical region referring to mountainous areas at the junction of three provinces of Anhui, Zhejiang and Jiangxi in China. The ancient name of this region is preserved for its beautiful landscape, rich cultural traditions and art heritage.

Huizhou is well known as "the countryside in pictures" for its distinctive vernacular architecture, the layout of village temples and walls of "horse-head" decorations. Building structures in this region are embellished everywhere with fascinating wood, brick and stone carvings.

◆ An Ancient Village in Huizhou

Huizhou Wood Carvings

The Hu Family Ancestral Temple at Longchuan village, Jixi County of Huizhou is known as the folk art museum full of wood carvings of different styles and rich themes. These exquisitely made wood carvings drew their artistic inspirations from local figures, landscape, animals, calligraphy and geometric patterns, and also embodied longings and good wishes from the local people for a happy life.

Huizhou wood carvings are made of local high-quality timbers and usually

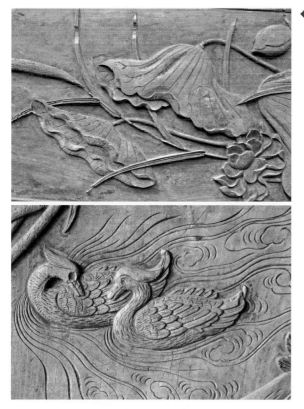

◆ Huizhou Wood Carvings
Huizhou wood carvings present detailed and complex images similar to paintings by incorporating different carving techniques of low, high, full and concave relief. Some pieces are carved and crafted up to 7-8 layers or more to create a three-dimensional effect.

◆ The Lion Wood Carving Statues in the House of Hu Zongxian
The lion wood carving statues in the house of Hu Zongxian, a high
official of the imperial court include a cub carved out at the bottom
to imply continuation of high-ranking positions in the family for
generations.

unvarnished to manifest the elegant natural wood grain. Once aged, the carved pieces

can gradually produce a protective layer of shining thin film. Only a few Huizhou wood

carvings are painted in simple colors such as red, black or gold in order to preserve the

simplistic style.

◆ The Wood Carving of Lotus Flowers on the Door in the Hu Family Ancestral Temple

Huizhou Stone Carvings

Located in a mountainous region, Huizhou abounds in rocks ideal for stone carvings. In ancient China stone carvings were not just decorations, but also symbols of the owner's social status. For example lion stone carvings in front of a residential courtyard were used to ward off evils and protect their house. The leopards were usually bestowed by the emperor to demonstrate that there was a prominent officer in the family with military honors.

Huizhou stone carvings are mostly stone reliefs or stone statues. The famous Xu Guo stone archway of She County is carved with images of dragons, lions, flying cranes

◆ Xu Guo Archway

◆ Huizhou Stone Carving "Seven Sages of the Bamboo Grove"

◆ Stone Carvings inside the Hu Family Ancestral Temple

and clouds. This stone structure is supported by columns that are secured by twelve stone lions at the bottom, of which eight lions stand on their hands. This was believed to use the principle of gravity to enhance the structure's stability. The stone leopard and three magpies on the archway represent the three consecutive promotions given by the imperial court to the archway's owner Xu Guo.

Huizhou stone carvings are commonly found on pillars, doors, walls, memorial archways and tombs. Their rare styles and shapes manifest Huizhou's splendid cultural tradition and ancient Chinese architecture.

Huizhou Brick Carvings

Huizhou brick carvings are usually found on door frames of gate towers and walls of court officials' residences or memorial temples. The front gate was considered as the face of a residence and always decorated with blue tiles and upturned eaves with brick carvings on pillar bases to show off the owner's wealth and taste. Upscale families often built a luxurious-looking "hanging-flower door," a special gate to separate external part from internal part of the courtyard. Both sides of the door were hung with suspended columns in the shape of petals which looked like hanging flowers.

Most Huizhou brick carvings have an elegant bluish gray color. Each carving artwork is an ensemble of as few as three or as many as nine engraved components. Popular large-scale carvings usually showcase mythical legends, local operas or folk stories. Other common themes include images of lions, elephants, tigers, and patterns of plum, orchid, bamboo, and chrysanthemum, and traditional auspicious patterns such as those from ancient utensils, imperial seals, and ceremonial scepters as well as auspicious Chinese characters.

◆ Brick Gate of Cheng Zhi Temple in Hong Village
This is a brick gate tower of a memorial temple in the village. Many Huizhou structures have a ceremonial gate made either from bricks or finely ground stones decorated with exquisite brick carvings on the door frames and drum-shaped rocks in the front.

◆ Huizhou Brick Carving *Bao Gong Inspecting Hometown*
This Huizhou brick carving depicts an inspection visit by Bao Gong, an ancient Chinese court official famous for his extreme honesty and uprightness.

◆ Huizhou Brick Carving *Town in Mountains*
This Huizhou brick carving depicts the streets and people of all walks of life in the center of a small town surrounded by mountains.

Tianjin Clay Figurine Zhang

In September 2013 the Number 8 Exhibition Hall of China Art Gallery in Beijing resounded with children's voice of excitement and camera shutter sound. They were looking at clay figurines on display from Tianjin. Can ordinary clay be made into artwork? In China clay figurine craftsmen are able to knead and sculpt pieces of clay into toys well-liked by children, and they can also build majestic clay statues.

Zhang Mingshan—The Crown of Clay Figurine Artists

"Clay Figure Zhang" of Tianjin is a famous folk art created by Zhang Mingshan (1826-1906) at the end of the Qing Dynasty. He was taught clay-sculpting skills as a child by his craftsman father. By the time he was a teenager, his clay figurines had already became very popular. They usually had long-lasting bright colors and vivid facial expressions, and would not chap after a long time. Known as the best of clay figurine craftsmen in both north and south, he is said to be able to chat while constructing a lifelike clay figure of the person he was talking to. His clay figurines once became a tribute to the

◆ Zhang Mingshan's Artwork "An Old Man with a Hat"

◆ "Clay Figure Zhang" Artwork

Qing imperial court. There was a saying that Empress Dowager Cixi of Qing preferred his clay figurines to gold figurines. After a few generations, Zhang clay figurines became one of the most representative works of China's clay art.

Zhang's achievements were not limited to the clay art; he also pioneered a new way of making an art available for common people. In ancient China, sculpture was mainly used for religious or memorial purposes. There was a custom of never making a figurine or a statue modeled on a live person. In order for people to accept his works, Zhang Mingshan created figurines with exaggerated expressions and a little distorted body shapes. Gradually his clay figurines went from temples into people's homes.

Different Faces of the Street Life

In addition to folklore, opera stories and literary works, Tianjin "Clay Figure Zhang" artworks also vividly depict the life of ordinary people from all walks of life. The typical example is a set of figurines called "Three Hundred Sixty Trades and Professions" created by Zhang Yuting from the second generation of Zhang family. This set reflects the life of real people on a city street market including a sugar blowing man, a carpenter, a stevedore, a foreteller, a candy peddler and a woman selling fish.

◆ "Clay Figure Zhang" Artwork "A Sugar Blowing Man"

◆ "Clay Figure Zhang" Painted Sculpture "The Carpenter"

Zhang clay figure art emphasizes portraying individual character by capturing the person's posture and expression at the moment. The technique and the artistry bring out a simple real-life visual effect to the clay figure. For example, the piece "Coming back from the Market" depicts an old woman wearing a pair of reading glasses weighing the fish she just bought from the market with a satisfied facial expression. Another example is "the Carpenter", which illustrates a carpenter at work with one eye closed and one eye open to adjust the tool.

Lovely Clay Dolls

A folk ballad said "when he cries, the child looks for his mother; and the mother buys a clay doll, and he is happy again." Clay dolls were one of the indispensable toys for children in old times.

Clay dolls vary in styles, each having its own local flavor. In Beijing, "Grandpa Rabbit" clay dolls are popular toys and decorations for the Mid-autumn Festival. It has a rabbit face with very long ears and a harelip, and a human body. In the old days street fairs in Beijing were full of vendors selling rabbit dolls of different sizes, a big attraction for children.

◆ "Grandpa Rabbit" Clay Doll

The famous "Big Happy Dolls" are the most unique work of Huishan clay figurines in Jiangsu Province. This doll has the look of a healthy plump baby boy and is dressed up in colorful silk costume, very adorable and pleasing. From this basic style Huishan clay artists have created other clay dolls such as the "Ruyi satisfying doll" and the "flower doll", a lovely smiling little girl, which inspired the creation of the "good luck doll" mascot for the 2008 Summer

◆ Huishan "Big Happy Doll"

Olympics in Beijing.

Xun County of Henan Province makes another kind of clay toys known as "clay cuckoos", which are tiny in size and hollow inside. Each figurine features a hole that can make a cuckoo sound when blown, hence the name. They are usually crafted into the shapes of human figures, birds, tigers, horses and roosters.

◆ "Clay Cuckoos"

Shaanxi Dough Art–"Flower Buns"

In North China, steamed buns, pita bread and noodles made from wheat are essential in everyday food. In Shaanxi, Shanxi and Shandong provinces, the dough used for bread and buns can also be sculpted into edible art pieces. Buns and breads with decorations are known as "flower buns."

◆ A Shaanxi "Flower Bun"

Edible Art

"Flower buns" are a Chinese traditional dough sculpting handicraft. Made mainly from wheat flour, the dough is kneaded into various shapes such as birds, fish, insects, vegetables, fruits and flowers, and decorated with black or red beans and dates, and then steamed and added food coloring. They are usually put on display and then consumed.

With vibrant colors and unique shapes, they represent good wishes for a happy life and become popular edible arrangements in the central and northern parts of Shaanxi.

◆ Shaanxi "Flower Bun" *Dragon and Phoenix Bring Prosperity*
The decorations on this Shaanxi "flower bun" include a dragon, the king of all animals and a phoenix, the queen of all birds. Together they symbolize harmony and good luck for the future in the Chinese traditional culture.

For example, the dough figurine "fish turning into a baby" has a baby's head and fish body, which is covered not with scales, but lotus flowers implying prosperity for future generations in the family.

Chinese New Year "Flower Buns"

"Flower buns" are the main food for the Chinese holidays. In Shaanxi, Shanxi and Shandong, buns decorated with dates are made for the Chinese New Year and buns in the shape of moon cakes for the Mid-autumn Festivals. On New Year's Eve, it is very common for a family to sit around the dinner table to enjoy the beauty and the taste of lavishly decorated "flower buns" while praying for the prosperity of the coming year.

"Flower buns" are also very popular at weddings and birthday celebrations as well as memorial ceremonies.

In Heyang County, Shaanxi Province, the bride must have a pair of beautifully

◆ Peasants in Shandong Province Are Making "Flower Buns" to Prepare for the Chinese New Year Celebrations

◆ Birthday "Peach Buns" of Longevity

decorated "flower buns" as part of her dowry to express the good wishes from her family to send their lovely daughter over to her husband's family for a happy life. In addition, included in her dowry is another pair of dough figurines of a boy and a girl to wish the young couple to have children soon. The "flower bun" arrangements for a wedding are so exquisite and elegant that the newlyweds, reluctant to eat them up, often display them as decorations in their new home.

When a baby boy is one month old, the wife's family would send over a "flower bun" shaped as a bull wishing him to be as strong as the bull. For a baby girl, the family would send a fish-shaped "flower bun" covered with dough flowers wishing her to have many children when she gets married.

For a senior's birthday celebration, younger generation would make peach-shaped buns, a concept similar to the birthday cake of western countries. The center of the bun usually has a big Chinese character "寿, means longevity" surrounded by images of cranes, pine leaves, and other auspicious patterns to wish the elderly a long and healthy life.

Dough Figurines

In the countryside, dough figurines are consumed after their display. But in the cities, dough artists paint their figurines directly after kneading and sculpting without having them steamed for the sole purpose of exhibiting them as art.

Dough figurines are well-liked by children. Composed mainly of wheat or glutinous rice flour, honey, water, paraffin and color, the soft dough mixture can be made into different shapes of human figures or animals by hand. A small stick is usually inserted in the back of the figure making it easier for children to hold it up. Most of the dough figurines are miniature sculptures of beautiful women, lovely children or characters from mythical legends, local operas or historical stories.

◆ A Stand of Dough Figurine at a Temple Fair

Paintings of China's Ethnic Minorities

China has fifty-five minority groups, each with its own distinctive culture, traditions and arts. Artworks of great vitality and creativity exist in many paintings from these ethnic minorities. The most creative and representative are Tibetan Thangka and Naxi Dongba pictographs.

Tibetan Thangka

With distinctive Tibetan characteristics and strong religious overtones, Thangka are Buddhist scroll paintings or picture panels depicting Tibetan Buddhist deities, stories, historical characters and Tibetan doctors.

Most Thangka are either made by appliqué or embroidery on silk (go-tang) or painted in color on garments (tson-tang). A Thangka must be made following definite and specific rules in color application. Red, blue, green, yellow and white are the main colors. Gold or black decorative lines are used to produce a three dimensional effect.

◆ Thangka "Manjushri Bodhisattva" [partial]

◆ Thangka "Sakyamuni and Eighteen Lohan" [partial]

Thanks to the large quantity of gold, silver, gems and other natural plant and mineral pigments applied, Thangka paintings can retain much of their lustrous and magnificent look even after a long period of time.

The process of making a Thangka is painstakingly complicated. To paint an eye requires at least 500 strokes. It usually takes from a few months up to a few years to complete the painting process for one Thangka. Varied in size, Thangka paintings are mostly vertical scrolls with a white space left at the bottom. The most common composition consists of a large Buddha image in the center and various religious images placed clockwise from the upper left corner all the way surrounding the centerpiece. These images include temples, palaces, rocks, clouds and trees.

Naxi Dongba Pictographs

Naxi is an ethnic group living in the Hengduan Mountains along the northwestern part of Yunnan Province and the southwestern part of Sichuan Province in China. Although it is a minority of a very small population, it is world. Famous for its unique Dongba culture, which originated from Dongba religion with a history of over 1,000 years. Dongba culture includes Dongba language, scripture, paintings, music and dance. Dongba religion is rooted in the belief of Naxi primitive polytheism; and their priests are called "Dongba" meaning "wise men" in their language.

◆ A Naxi Woodblock Painting

◆ "The Road to Heaven" [partial]

As an important aspect of Dongba culture, Dongba paintings depict religious gods and demons based on Naxi's belief and their daily activities. In ancient times Dongba artists would paint images of Buddha, deities, animals, plants, or demons for people to worship during sacrificial ceremonies. The styles of Dongba paintings include woodblock paintings, scripture cover illustrations, paper card paintings and scroll paintings. "The Road to Heaven" is the most famous Dongba scroll painting, which consists of over 100 strips in four parts describing the hell, the human world, nature and heaven with a total of 360 colorful and uniquely shaped figures and animal images.

Today some young Naxi artists, while incorporating the quintessence of Dongba traditional art, have successfully applied modern techniques and materials to create impressive artworks with rich connotations, which vividly demonstrate the history and unique customs of the Naxi people.

◆ "The Road to Heaven" Relief in the Garden of Dongba Gods, Lijiang of Yunnan Province

The World's Only Surviving Hieroglyphs

Known as the language "living fossil", the Dongba language is the only surviving hieroglyphic language in the world today. There are about 1,400 glyphs, each representing a physical object or an abstract idea. They are often combined to record complicated events. In the 1920s the Dongba language caught the attention of the academic world both in China and abroad. Jacques Bacot, a French scholar examined 370 Dongba glyphs in his book "Mexie Studies" and Dr. Joseph F. Rock from the United States compiled a two-volume "Naxi-English Encyclopedia Dictionary." In 2003 ancient Naxi Dongba literature manuscripts were accepted into the UNESCO "Memory of the World Register".

◆ Ancient Naxi Dongba Literature Manuscripts

Folk Crafts

Jingdezhen Porcelain

Situated in the northeastern part of Jiangxi Province, Jingdezhen is well-known in China and abroad as the "capital of porcelain" for its high-quality porcelain ware.

Blue-and-white porcelain first came out as early as in the 13th century in Jingdezhen, which later became the porcelain making center in China by the 14th century. Today porcelain production is still prosperous in this ancient city of many old-time kilns along the river and porcelain workshops in downtown. The presence of porcelain is evident in homes in the blue flagstone paved alleys and along the streets with blue-and-white decorated streetlights.

What is Blue-and-white Porcelain

Blue-and-white porcelain is a kind of special white pottery decorated under the glaze of cobalt oxide blue pigments. The design is applied using the Chinese traditional ink

◆ Blue-and-white Porcelain Jar "Guiguzi Down the Hills" (Yuan Dynasty)
Guiguzi was an important strategist in the Warring States Period. This porcelain jar depicts a beautiful landscape with the historical figure Guiguzi against a background of shining Blue-and-white patterns.

painting technique to produce an elegant visual effect of strong contrast between the bluish patterns and the shining glaze. The color is very stable and difficult to wear out. As a result blue-and-white ware is a favorite of art collectors worldwide for its high artistic values.

At the award ceremony of the 2008 Beijing Olympic water sports, the Chinese trophy girls were dressed in gowns with blue-and-white porcelain patterns, which became the most popular style of the five Beijing Olympics dresses chosen for award ceremonies.

◆ The Ceremonial Dress of Blue-and-White Porcelain Design for the 2008 Beijing Olympics

Porcelain Wares for the Imperial Family

Porcelain wares had always been popular not only among commoners, but also emperors and their families in China since ancient times.

Jingdezhen started to produce imperial porcelain wares since Tang and Song Dynasties. The designs and styles were often changed based on the aesthetic taste of different emperors in a thousand years

◆ Blue-and-White Porcelain of Interlaced Flower Patterns (Ming Dynasty)

◆ Scenery of Jingdezhen

of porcelain production history. In the Northern Song Dynasty (1004), the Queen of the Liao Kingdom in the north led her army to attack the capital of Song in the south. The Song emperor tried to negotiate for peace by promising a large amount of gold, silver and other treasures for Liao. But the offer was rejected by the Liao Queen, who instead asked for 200,000 pieces of Chinese porcelain ware in three months. The Song emperor immediately ordered Jingdezhen to make these wares. In two months after day and night production, 300,000 blue-and-white wares of different designs came out from Jingdezhen. Eventually the Liao army retreated to the north and the Song Dynasty recovered the lost land. During the Ming and Qing Dynasties, porcelain wares produced in Jingdezhen were regarded as "state porcelain". Jingdezhen also manufactured 7,000 porcelain wares for the wedding of Emperor Tongzhi of Qing.

Porcelain in the West

Invented in China, porcelain became the most typical symbol of the Chinese culture, and the earliest bridge between China and the rest of the world, which was captured by its beauty.

In the 17th century, royal families of Western Europe started to collect porcelain ware from China. Jingdezhen immediately turned into the world's porcelain production center. A 1610 book about the kingdom of Portugal claimed that the Chinese porcelain was the most beautiful object discovered, much more precious than gold and silver. Chinese porcelain wares were displayed in churches, palaces and

◆ Porcelain Tea Cup with a Lid Painted with Plum Flowers of Ink-painting Style against a Yellow Background. (Republic of China)

◆ Porcelain Tea Pot of Gilded Flower Patterns Outlined
in Red with a Pagoda Image (Qing Dynasty)

mansions throughout Europe. Louis XIV and XV of France fell in love
with Chinese porcelain advocating embracing these wares into the
French daily life. When France was in huge debt, Louis XV couldn't
bear to sell his porcelain collection, and would rather produce currency
out of melted gold and silver wares. When large quantities of Chinese
porcelain wares entered the European market, they became very
popular even in ordinary citizens' homes. An afternoon tea with a set
of porcelain ware was considered as a symbol of a higher standard
of living. British Queen Mary II was also fascinated with the Chinese
porcelain and built many glass cabinets to display her collection in the
palace. The British simply called any porcelain from China "Chinaware".

Techniques of Making Blue-and-white Porcelain

After almost a thousand years of exploration and practice, ancient Chinese porcelain artisans developed a highly organized production process for the world renown pottery ware.

The basic operations included selecting materials, crushing, cleaning, forming the clay, glazing and finally firing the formed clay bodies. Every operation involved many complicated steps and any misstep could result in the poor quality of the final product. For example, finely crushed material had to pass through a series of screens to remove any under-sized or over-sized particles and the cleaned clay pieces were later combined with water to produce the desired consistency. Magnetic filtration was then used to remove iron from these watery mixtures. The cleaned slurry went through a glazing operation for proper coating before the clay was poured into molds for the desired shape.

◆ An Ancient Kiln Site in Jingdezhen

Illustrations of Blue-and-white Porcelain Making Process

◆ Forming

In soft forming the clay is first shaped by wheel throwing, in which the potter places the desired amount of body on a wheel and shapes it while the wheel turns.

◆ Pressing

Pressing is used to compact and shape the clay paste into the corresponding mold. This step involves applying pressure first to the bottom layer of the paste using a wooden strip and then equally to all sides of the body by hand to make it fully consistent with the mold.

◆ Trimming

After pressing, the clay body is let dry in the shade and trimmed to the desired shape or thickness with a knife.

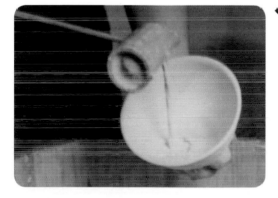

◆ Glazing

Glaze is a mixture of alumina, calcia and other silicate minerals. Different types of glazes can be produced by varying the proportions of the constituent ingredients. Glazing is then applied to the ware by means of painting, pouring, dipping, or spraying under high temperature to achieve a glassy coating on the body. Glazing enables the porcelain ware's thermal and chemical stability and water resistance.

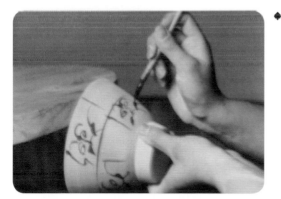

◆ Painting

Yuan Dynasty's blue-and-white patterns were generally painted, sketched or dipped onto the body with a high-quality brush of a pointed tip using different shades of cobalt-blue pigment.

Porcelain Applications in Daily Life

In ancient China porcelain wares were not only artworks for appreciation, but also the most common utensils in people's daily life. A thousand years' porcelain history saw the rise of a great variety of porcelain styles including incense burners, pots, inkstone, pillows, bowls, cups and bottles.

Today porcelain is still irreplaceable in people's daily life. The majority of the Chinese dishware, wine and tea sets, and other vessels are made of porcelain. New technology has been used together with the traditional handicraft techniques to develop

◆ Modern Blue Porcelain Tea Set

◆ Modern Porcelain Decoration

more modern designs and shapes. Inorganic ingredients are added to the raw material to make porcelain wares more durable and beautiful.

Chinese porcelain designs, especially the blue-and-white patterns have been applied to other areas such as fashion, furniture and gift packaging. In recent years, blue-and-white porcelain elements have frequently emerged in the world's fashion designs. In 2005, Roberto Cavalli, an Italian fashion designer used Chinese blue porcelain floral compositions in his fall fashion series. In 2011 American Rodarte's collection of silk-chiffon dresses showed off the elegant and exquisite design of Chinese porcelain patterns. In 2013 the famous Italian fashion brand Valentino vividly demonstrated the beauty of the blue-and-white porcelain designs in his fall and winter collections.

Leather Carved Figures– Shadow Puppetry

Shadow puppetry is an ancient form of entertainment. Some people believe that it was the predecessor of present-day motion pictures.

In some aspects, the Chinese shadow play is similar to a motion picture, both being an art form of lights and shadows on the screen. But a shadow play is a live performance where the puppeteer makes the puppet talk, sing or act directly from behind the curtain to tell a story.

The shadow play might be the first theater art from China to be known by the world. In 1781 the famous German writer Goethe invited a shadow puppetry troop to his birthday party giving his guests a very pleasant surprise.

Moving Paper Cuts

Shadow puppetry, also known as "light puppetry", is a Chinese storytelling folk entertainment performed by puppeteers controlling leather or paper cut-out figures held between a source of light and a translucent screen. In China it is also regarded as the earliest form of movies.

Shadow puppets look like moving paper-cut figures. What are they made of? They are usually made from animal skins such as sheep, cattle or donkey. After it

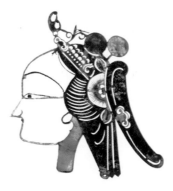

◆ The Head of a Shadow Puppet

◆ Shadow Puppetry Performance

is soaked, crusted, stretched and dried until translucent, the supple leather is then ready for tracing the puppet silhouette and cutting it out. The head, chest, waist, hands and legs of each puppet have to be made separately in order to allow the puppet's free movement. It takes over 3,000 cuts to make a puppet. Pigment is then applied to the cut-out puppet. In order to have full control of the puppet's movement, a manipulation rod is added to the finished puppet.

◆ The Backstage of a Shadow Play

Various Shadow Puppet Models

◆ *A Folk Variety Show Troop*

◆ Genie Shadow Puppets

◆ *Mu Guiying*
It is a traditional shadow play about the Yang family of generals in the Song Dynasty.

◆ *Wu Family Village*
It is a traditional shadow play about the story of a Tang Dynasty general re-uniting with his wife.

Puppet Artists of Multiple Roles

In the Chinese countryside, the shadow puppet performance is nicknamed as "a show of five busy people", meaning that it only takes five puppeteers to perform a complete show. The master puppeteer is responsible for controlling the movements of the puppets and the rest four people have to play 16 different musical instruments. Every one of them has to be well-equipped with multiple skills to be able to run the whole show. They must be able to move the puppets, sing and play musical instruments. They are described as having "a mouth that can tell a thousand years of stories and two hands that can command a million soldiers". The key to make a shadow come alive relies on the skills of the master puppeteer to handle the movements of the puppets. He must comfortably operate the control mechanism for each puppet based on the content of the show.

◆ The Backstage of a Shadow Play

Contemporary Shadow Puppetry Art

In ancient times shadow plays were very popular in China's rural areas similar to today's movies and TV shows. As the main form of entertainment for over a thousand years, shadow plays brought a magic world of lights and shadows to adults and children in villages after dark. Shadow plays, also known as "happy shadows", played an essential role in holidays, weddings, ceremonies of good harvests, birthday parties and openings of new businesses. Sometimes the show would continue for three days on end. Most plays were about legendary heroes fighting against evils.

Today few people go to watch a shadow play in the theater due to the rapid growth of movies, TV and online media. Chinese shadow puppet artists have been exploring new ways to revive this traditional art form. In the 1960s a series of animated movies were made using shadow puppets and Chinese paper cut figures, and they were well received by children. In the 2006 Chinese New Year gala sponsored by the China Central Television 12 seniors and 24 children performed the shadow dance "Pretty Aged Women", which became a hit on TV. Shadow plays began to show new vitality as a form of performing art.

◆ Shadow Dance *Pretty Aged Women*

Puppetry

Puppets are toy figures or animals made from wood or fabric. Manipulated by puppeteers, they can give all kinds of performances. As an entertainment especially well-liked by children, puppet shows are very popular in the world. China also has different types of puppets including string, wooden rod, wire and hand puppets.

Ever-lasting Puppet Shows

Chinese puppetry originated approximately around the Han Dynasty. Some master puppeteers started to perform in theaters specifically set up for puppet shows by the Song Dynasty. After the Yuan Dynasty, widely popular puppet plays developed into distinctive styles in different regions and by different schools of puppetry.

In recent decades, Chinese puppetry grew from a folk art into a more specialized art form with emergence of new stories, performing styles and contemporary figures made by modern carving techniques. Chinese puppet troops were sent abroad to perform and participate in cultural exchanges with puppeteers from other countries.

In the late 1940s the first Chinese puppet movie "An Emperor's Dream" came out, followed by "Magic Pen" and "Smart Goat". In 1958 Taiwan produced its first hand

◆ String Puppets

Every move of a string puppet is suspended and controlled by a number of strings attached to the head, back, waist, arms, hands and toes. String puppets are the most flexible of all puppet types. They can perform sophisticated moves such as hair combing, hair throwing, flute playing, fan waving and even creating magic illusions on the stage.

◆ Rod Puppets

There are three wooden rods controlling a puppet, two attached to the hands and one supporting the head and the body. The puppeteer manipulates the puppet's movement and facial expressions by operating the three rods. Because the puppeteer has to raise the puppet up above his head to perform, rod puppets are also known as "lifted puppets" in China.

◆ Hand Puppets

Hand puppets are also known as bag puppets in China, the name deriving from the puppet's bag-like costume. The puppet is operated by one hand which occupies the interior of the puppet with the forefinger controlling the puppet's head, and the other four fingers controlling the two hands. Hand puppet masters are known for performing difficult acrobats such as jar balancing on the head, multiple plates spinning, archery, fire spitting, and dragon and lion dancing. The puppet can demonstrate a lively facial expression with a movable mouth and eyelids on the wood-carved head.

◆ Wire Puppets

This kind of puppet is relatively small in size, about 20-40 centimeters long. The movement of the body and the two hands of a puppet is controlled by hard wires. Usually the puppet is placed in a transparent box so that people can watch from all four sides how the puppet turns his head or body, runs around, spins a plate, lights a candle, pours wine and waves a fan.

puppet movie "Journey to the West". These new creations expanded the puppet shows' content to children's literature, military life and mythical legends, and greatly enhanced the expressiveness of the traditional puppetry.

The Making of Chinese Puppets

Exquisitely made Chinese puppets are not only props in the traditional theatrical stage, but also highly anesthetic handicrafts. As most of them are modeled after the characters in the Chinese local operas, these puppets usually present colorful exaggerated images.

The world of puppets has thousands of shapes and varieties. The basic methods of constructing a puppet are similar, generally including the six steps of making the head, the hat, costume, the body, shoes and control mechanism. The head is the most important representing the character's unique image and personality. It is usually made from hard wood. Making a puppet head involves four steps: carving, installing control mechanism, painting and polishing. Some puppet heads are made of clay for quicker and low-cost construction, a method popular in the northwestern regions.

◆ A Rod Puppet Mask from a Local Opera Made in Xiaoyi, Shanxi Province

◆ Zhangzhou Puppet Show

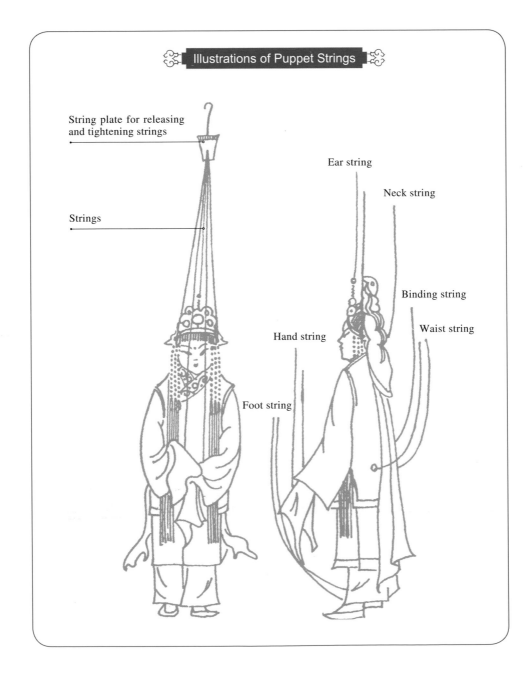

Illustrations of Puppet Strings

String plate for releasing and tightening strings

Strings

Ear string

Neck string

Binding string

Waist string

Hand string

Foot string

Puppet Show Customs

In ancient China people lived a primitive agrarian life spending most of their time farming. Lively and humorous puppet shows became an important entertainment for them in slack seasons. They were also present in holidays, weddings and birthday celebrations to promote festivity. In Putian, Nan'an and Yongchun of Fujian Province, it is still a custom to have puppet shows performed for weddings. Usually the puppet show starts at the midnight of the day before the wedding when the master puppeteer sings to bless the newlyweds in the celebration ceremony. In the northeastern part of Fujian, people invite puppeteers to lead praying for longevity in the birthday ceremony for an elderly in the family.

Afterwards everybody will watch puppet shows related to birthday celebrations. In the southern part of Fujian puppet shows are performed in a ritual to pray for safety before the construction of a new house or a new bridge starts.

◆ A Puppet Show from South of Fujian Province

Yixing Clay Teapot

Everybody in China knows tea and every tea lover in China is familiar with Yixing clay teapots, also known as purple clay teapots.

Purple Clay Teapots and Tea

● What is a purple clay teapot?

It is a type of tea set, an artwork and a culture in China.

Purple clay teapots appeared about 800 years ago and very soon rose to the best of all teapots. They became the top choice of tea sets for Chinese literati after the Ming Dynasty. A tea aficionado, Emperor Qianlong of the Qing Dynasty always brought along several purple clay tea sets on his trips. Starting from his reign, Yixing purple clay teapots had always been sent to the imperial court as a tribute.

Purple clay teapots entered Western Europe at the end of the Qing Dynasty following a large amount of tea export. They immediately aroused great interest from the Europeans. Soon Chinese clay tea sets began to sell in large quantities to Western Europe, Japan, Mexico and other South American countries. Many craftsmen in other countries tried unsuccessfully to reproduce Chinese clay teapots due to an important fact that the clay for this kind of teapots only came from Yixing, China.

Yixing Clay

Situated in the south of Jiangsu Province, Yixing is a small, but culturally famous city of over 2,000 years' history and 7,000 years of pottery making. Known as the thousand-year old capital of pottery, the people in Yixing have always been living on the unique type of clay abundantly available in this region. Approximately formed between 200-400 million years ago, the clay, known as the purple clay and the best of all clay types, can produce wares of rich color and a smooth surface with an excellent balance between flexibility and firmness after being fired. Clay teapots made here were named after the purple clay.

Purple clay teapots are treasured for their ability to enhance the flavor, aroma and texture of tea. The porous nature of the clay allows the teapot to absorb the essence of tea. If it is used only for one type of tea for a long time, the teapot can still generate the tea aroma in hot water even without tea leaves.

◆ A Yixing Potter is Washing and Extracting Pure Purple Clay in the River

Hand Therapy with Clay Teapot

It is believed that when tea is being brewed in a clay teapot, the temperature will reach 50 to 80 degrees Celsius, ideal for improving blood flow and circulation of the hands. In addition, moving the hands over the surface of the teapot covered with many uneven clay particles can also function as a good hand therapy.

◆ Hand Therapy Using a Purple Clay Teapot

The Making of Purple Clay Teapots

The birth of every purple clay teapot requires a dozen to several dozens of complicated processes through different instruments and techniques. Generally wet clay is first crushed into very fine pieces of uniform thickness, which will then be molded into various parts of the teapot. The parts are patted together and polished to form the teapot body, which will be fired in a kiln.

In ancient times, clay teapots were fired in brick kilns called "dragon kilns" built on the hillside slopes. These curved tunnels of 30-70 meters long looked like dragons, hence the name "dragon kilns". It was described that the flame coming out of these kilns lit up the whole sky every night in Yixing in the old days when teapots had to be fired for 24 hours. Artisans made the decision when to turn off the fire by observing the changes of the teapots through a window on the kiln. The success or failure of the entire kiln of teapots depended solely on the experience and wisdom of the artisans.

Today it only takes several hours to fire a kiln of teapots with modern equipment and technology. But handmade purple clay teapots still have an indispensable place in the heart of the teapot artists and connoisseurs.

◆ A Purple Clay Tea Set

Steps to Make a Round Clay Teapot

Cut crushed clay into strips;

Pat strips into pieces of uniform thickness;

Construct parts for the teapot mouth and the bottom;

Pound pieces to remove any excess air bubbles;

Make an even and smooth surface;

Cut off excess parts;

Pat finished clay pieces into a slab and roll the slab into a cylinder shape;

Use a bamboo tool to connect and smooth the connected two sides;

Turn the wheel to pat the bottom into the required curvature;

Install the bottom part and pat the lower body into the required arc surface; use a small bamboo strip to cut excess clay off the bottom;

Pat the upper body into the required arc surface;

Use a sharp iron tool to make a rough shape of the teapot sprout;

Use a bamboo strip to finish shaping and cut out the teapot sprout and the handle;

Attach the teapot sprout and handle onto the body;

Press soft clay strips into the mold for the lid; pat inside of the lid into convex arc and smooth the surface;

Secure decorative edges on the lid, cut off excess and smooth the edges;

Shape the lid cover into an arc surface.

Poetry, Paintings and Purple Clay Teapots

Design patterns on these teapots demonstrate perfectly the Chinese arts and literature including poetry, flowers, birds, landscaping paintings, and portraits of ancient figures. Many inscriptions on teapots are about tea or plants from well-known ancient poets and writers. Blending sculpture, painting, poetry, calligraphy and seal carving all in one artwork makes purple clay teapots stand out in the Chinese folk crafts.

The teapots inscribed by famous calligraphers are known as "masterpiece teapots" among teapot connoisseurs. These teapots emerged in the Ming and Qing Dynasties. Famous calligraphers such as Dong Xichang, Zheng Banqiao, Chen Mansheng, Ren Bonian and Wu Changshuo had all collaborated with teapot artists to have their calligraphy inscribed on teapots. Well-known contemporary painters such as Huang Binhong, Ya Ming, Tang Yun and Cheng Shifa also left their work and calligraphy on these masterpiece teapots.

◆ Masterpiece Teapots

Master of Arts

Purple clay teapots are well-known for enhancement of tea taste, elegant shapes and most of all, the artistry which blends Chinese traditional culture and arts of poetry, calligraphy, paintings and seals into one artwork.

Teapot artists often decorate their teapots with poetry, calligraphy, paintings or auspicious patterns. Many have their names inscribed on the inside or bottom of the teapot. Some collaborate with cultural celebrities to create artistic teapots, which have become popular collectable items of high artistic values.

◆ Different Types of Purple Clay Teapots

◆ It is believed that the purple clay teapots are best for Wulong tea.

Auspicious Chinese Knots

In 2012 the Chinese "Shenzhou 10" spacecraft brought back a red decorative Panchang knot hung in the Tiangong-1 trial space laboratory module. This was the only decorative item in the lab in addition to the national flag.

Chinese knotting is an ancient folk handicraft, which can construct a variety of knotting patterns with one cord. Panchang knots are only one design out of many.

Culture of Chinese Knotting

The majority of Chinese women in ancient times were illiterate, but they must know embroidery and knotting. One cord could quickly turn into a beautiful knot in their hands. A knot could be tied in different ways and different knotting patterns could come from the same design. Chinese women in ancient times expressed their feelings and longings for a happy life through their needlework and knotting, which were an essential part of their life.

The Chinese word for knotting is an emotionally charged term. It sounds similar to the word for auspiciousness representing blessings, and it means linkages, being connected, unity and together forever representing closeness, unification and harmony.

The word is also often used to describe a marriage. Decorative knots are exchanged between a man and a woman as tokens of love. The "heart to heart" knot has always been the symbol of love between a man and a woman. Decorative knots in China not only demonstrate elegant and harmonious design patterns, but also people's love of truth, goodness, beauty and their desire and pursuit for a harmonious society.

◆ Panchang Knot Decorative Accessory

Event Recording with Knots

To help memorize things, ancient Chinese used different ways to document events and knotting was one of the early methods. They would tie knots according to the nature, size and quantity of the event. For example, a big knot represented a big event, and vice versa. They would tie a knot in the shape of grains to record the grains' growth. There were also knots to document weather changes. One-cord knots represented simple numbers and multiple cross knots meant for more complicated things.

◆ Ancient Knots for Recording Events

Knot Decorations

Chinese knots have been used as belts or decorative ornaments. Some of the earliest evidence of knotting was found extensively on ancient utensils, garments, hats and accessories. The Ming and Qing Dynasties witnessed very advanced and sophisticated knotting techniques. Knots of exquisite and intricate tying patterns were seen in many

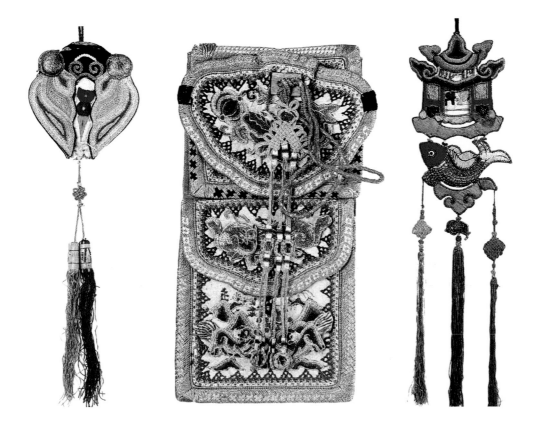

◆ Various Knot Ornaments

daily necessities such as sedan chairs, curtains, lanterns, hooks, fans, belts, flute accessories, hairpins, flower baskets, sachets, purses, glass cases and tobacco pouches. Also emerged at the time were the dazzling ever-changing combination knots of many styles.

Today, the Chinese still like knot decorations and ornaments. During the Chinese New Year celebrations, people would hang a few red knots to enhance the festivity. In their daily life people wear colorful knot accessories on their clothes, decorate gift packages or place them in their homes as decorations.

◆ Knot Decorations for the Chinese New Year Celebrations

How to Make Simple Chinese Knots

A small knot shows the wisdom, techniques and creativity of ancient Chinese people. It looks simple, but tying it requires some efforts. The cord or the ribbon may be round, square, flat or of double colors. Twisting it or tying it to the wrong direction will lead to failure. How to pull the cord, where to pull it and whether to pull it hard or softly will result in different shapes of knots.

The following introduces some simple steps to tie two types of Chinese knots: the Panchang knot and the "heart-to-heat" knot. Give it a try.

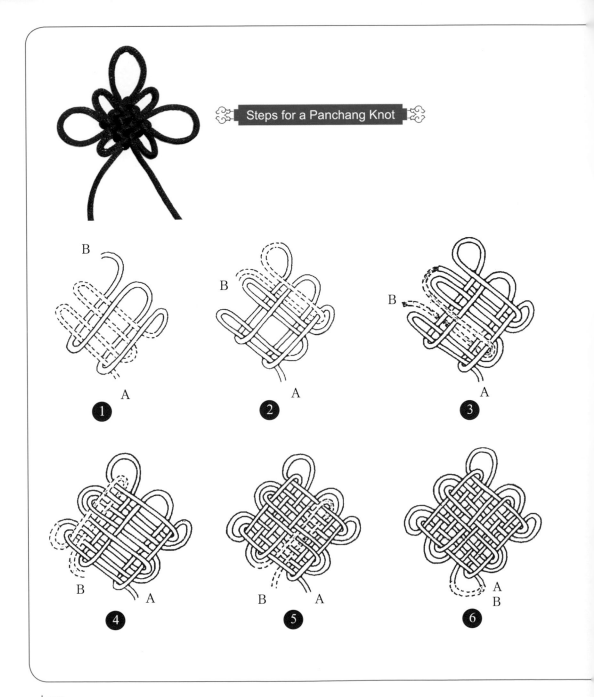

Steps for a Panchang Knot

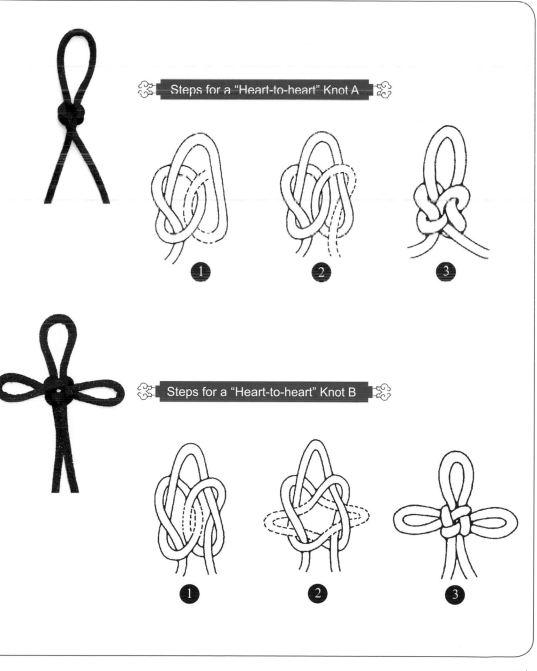

Steps for a "Heart-to-heart" Knot A

1

2

3

Steps for a "Heart-to-heart" Knot B

1

2

3

◆ Chinese Knots

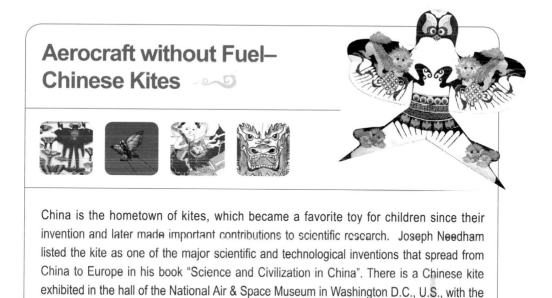

Aerocraft without Fuel— Chinese Kites

China is the hometown of kites, which became a favorite toy for children since their invention and later made important contributions to scientific research. Joseph Needham listed the kite as one of the major scientific and technological inventions that spread from China to Europe in his book "Science and Civilization in China". There is a Chinese kite exhibited in the hall of the National Air & Space Museum in Washington D.C., U.S., with the description "The earliest aerocraft of human beings are the kites and rockets of China".

The Earliest Aerocraft in the World

The Chinese began to make kites as early as in the Spring-autumn and Warring States Periods 2,000 years ago. The kite was built in the shape of a bird using bamboo for a strong and lightweight framework and silk or paper for sail material. In the wind the air flow lifted the kite and sustained it in flight. The kite became the earliest aerocraft in the world. Gradually flying kites grew into a very popular outdoor recreational activity. In spring and autumn, people would come out and fly kites. In history kites had also been used in military operations, communication and surveying.

Kite artists express people's longings for happiness, longevity, auspiciousness and avoidance of disasters through kite designs and decorative patterns, making kites not only beautiful, but also a symbol of good luck. People hope that the flying kite can take their wishes up in the sky; the higher the kite flies, the sooner their wishes can come true. In most regions in China kite flying activity is popular in spring and autumn, mainly because of the wind and the traditional farming seasons. The wind in spring and autumn is steady and moderate, suitable for kite flying. In the traditional agricultural China entertainment and recreational activities are usually carried out in slack seasons.

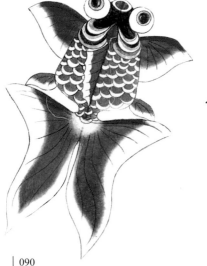

◆ Kites

In 1915 China participated in the Panama-Pacific International Exposition for the first time. Kite masters Ha Changying from Bejing and Wei Yuantai from Tianjin won a gold medal and a silver medal respectively. After 1949 kite flying competitions emerged in many areas of China promoting the folk art of kites to a new level. The world largest kite "the Mollusk Octopus" made by the Chinese weighing 200 kilograms and measuring 1500 square meters was successfully launched in October 2013 at the International Kite Festival in Zhuhai.

◆ Flying Kites

Making a Simple Kite

An exquisitely made kite is an object of art valuable for appreciation and collection. In 1915 it was the first time that Chinese kites were displayed in the Panama-Pacific International Exposition and China won a gold medal. That gold-medal kite went through dozens of production processes including design, material selection, framing, constructing, cutting, painting, assembling, tying the kite string, test flying and adjustment. Making a simple kite for recreational purposes is a lot simpler. The basic steps include:

◆ An Artist Is Painting a Kite

1. Frame the bamboo strips into the kite shape already designed.

2. Cover the frame with paper or fabric.

3. Paint patterns on the paper or the fabric.

4. Attach the string and the kite is ready.

It is easier to fly a kite with two people in collaboration. One person stands against the wind, unwinds several meters of the string and holds the back of the kite. The other person pulls on the string to launch the kite in a gust of wind and runs while releasing more string as the kite flies into the air. Once the kite rises to a certain height, adjust the string back and forth to make the kite fly steadily.

Weaving and Dyeing of China's Minorities

In the traditional Chinese garment making process, raw materials of linen, silk, wool and cotton must be first spun into threads, woven into fabric, then color dyed, printed with patterns and finally sewn into clothes. Chinese weaving and dyeing techniques are rich in variety and well-developed over the course of thousands of years. Demonstrating the most distinctive features are dyeing and weaving handicrafts from some ethnic minorities such as Tujia brocade, Tibetan Pulu, Miao batik and Bai tie-dye.

Tujia Brocade

The Tujia, one of the largest ethnic minorities in China, live in areas across the common borders of Hunan, Hubei, Sichuan and Guizhou Provinces. The Tujia is well known for their farming and weaving skills and Tujia brocade is considered to be one of the three best brocade arts in China.

◆ Tujia Brocade

The Tujia brocade has a history of over a thousand years. The main materials used for the Tujia classic brocades are silk, cotton and wool yarns. Tujia women weave the patterns from the back of the brocade. This method produces brocades with a solid and durable structure, beautiful patterns on both sides and bright long-lasting colors. The quintessence of Tujia brocades is represented by the sharp contrast of the colors, black against white, red against green and blue against yellow.

Xilankapu is a special kind of Tujia brocade style, known for its vibrant colors and unique patterns. It is hand woven with red, yellow, blue, white and black threads going lengthwise and across to create over 120 gorgeous patterns such as moon, sun and stars in the sky, and images of animals and flowers. Tujia girls start to learn how to weave Xilankapu when they are twelve or thirteen years old to prepare for their wedding dress and ornaments for their dowry. The Tujia people also like to wear a decorative brocade shawl over their costumes for holiday celebrations.

◆ Tujia Brocade

Zhuang is an ethnic minority with a long history living for generations in the southwestern provinces of Guangxi, Yunnan, Guizhou and Hunan. Zhuang brocade is the most unique and well-known handicraft of this ethnic group.

Produced by interwoven silk and cotton threads, Zhuang brocade has a bold artistic style with structured argyle geometric patterns and strong color contrast. The durability and softness give Zhuang brocade high practical values, excellent for making quilt covers, tablecloths, handbags, and aprons. Zhuang brocades have also developed into large-size wall artworks for modern interior decorations. Today the Zhuang people still keep the tradition of making brocade quilt covers for newlyweds and brocade straps for carrying babies.

◆ A Zhuang Woman Works on a Brocade Weaving Machine

Tibetan Pulu

Tibetans live in a plateau region of high altitude, cold weather and harsh natural conditions and depend on nomadic animal husbandry and agriculture. To survive and adapt to the life on the plateau, both Tibetan men and women wear Pulu robes.

Tibetan Pulu is a type of handmade wool fabric used mainly for making Tibetan clothing. It is durable, thick, thermal, wind resistant and waterproof. Making Pulu involves combing the wool, twisting wool threads, weaving and dyeing. The Pulu is first produced in white and later dyed in different colors.

For the convenience and flexibility required for their nomadic life style, long robes worn by Tibetans are spacious so that arms can move freely inside. Not only can they keep the body warm, they are also easy to take off and put on for traveling. At nighttime it can turn into a sleeping bag by untying the belt and taking off the sleeves, and using half of the robe as bed sheet and the other half the cover. On a hot summer day, one can slip an arm out of a sleeve and leave one shoulder bare to release the heat. This style of leaving the right shoulder and arm free is a unique feature of Tibetan dressing tradition.

◆ Tibetan Pulu Belt

◆ A Tibetan Woman in a Tibetan Robe

Miao Batik

The Miao ethnic group live primarily in Guizhou, Hunan, Hubei, Sichuan, Yunnan Provinces and Guangxi Zhuang Autonomous Region. With over a thousand years' history batik is the most famous Miao's well-known handicraft among embroidery, brocade, batik and paper cutting.

The making process of this ancient tradition of printing and dyeing includes these basic steps: heating and melting a mixture of proportional white and yellow wax as well as rosin to create a liquid wax; using the liquid wax to apply patterns on the fabric; immersing the fabric in a vat of dye; and finally when the dyeing process

◆ Miao Batik Children's Clothing

is completed, washing the fabric in hot water to dissolve the wax in order to reveal the patterns in white color on the dyed fabric. The Miao use a thin blade of a bronze knife to dispense the hot wax and draw patterns on the white fabric. Then indigo plants grown by the Miao are mixed in a big jar, in which the white fabric with hot wax is dyed. A special technique to drip the hot wax slowly onto the fabric is very popular among the Miao. They first place a thin plate carved with different patterns over the white cloth and pour hot wax onto the plate before the fabric is dyed. At the end of the process the fabric is washed in boiling water to dissolve the wax in order to bring the blue-and-white patterns out. Most Miao batik designs are natural and geometric patterns of animals and plants, jaggedness, stars, clouds and meander border.

Yao Batik

The Yao ethnic group mainly reside in the mountainous terrain of Hunan, Yunnan, Guangdong and Guizhou Provinces and Guangxi Autonomous Region. Yao women are good at handicrafts of weaving, printing, dyeing and embroidery. The costumes they make have bright and vibrant colors.

The Yao mainly use batik for printing and dyeing. The method is to sandwich the fabric in between two wooden boards engraved with patterns. Then melted wax is poured onto the patterns on the wooden boards and then fabric is dyed in indigo. The wax is removed after the fabric is dried. The finished product is referred to as the "Yao pattern fabric" known for its fineness and strong color contrast.

In order to make it durable and the color long lasting, Yao women will go through one final step to soak the fabric in a cowhide or porcine blood solution, and steam and dry it multiple times. It is believed that the fabric processed in this way can have an anti-inflammatory effect on the skin.

◆ Yao Costumes

Tie Dyeing of Bai Ethnic Minority

The Bai ethnic minority mainly live in the Bai Autonomous Prefecture of Yunnan Province. Tie-dyed products are very popular in this region. The technique is to use linen, silk and cotton threads to tie and knot the fabric neatly and tightly and then soak the fabric in a vat of indigo dye. Different ways of tying and knotting produce different

◆ A Bai Woman Is Tie Dyeing Some Fabric

◆ A Bai Tie-dyeing Workshop

patterns in the undyed spots on the fabric. After the tie dyeing process, the fabric shows natural and elegant white floral patterns against the blue background. This design demonstrates the hardworking, simple and honest characteristics of the Bai people.

Most Bai tie-dyeing designs come from commonly seen animals and plants such as bees, caterpillars, butterflies and delicate flowers. The lively and natural blue-and-white patterns are used extensively in fashion designs and household decorations. There are over 200 popular design patterns used by the local Bai women. Almost every one of them is able to tie-dye a dozen patterns.

◆ Contemporary Bai Tie-dyed Products